The Beatitude of Mercy

Love Watches over Justice

✠ ✠ ✠

WIPF & STOCK · Eugene, Oregon

Terry A. Veling

Wipf and Stock Publishers
199 W 8th Ave, Suite 3
Eugene, OR 97401

The Beatitude of Mercy
Love Watches Over Justice
By Veling, Terry A.
Copyright©2010 by Veling, Terry A.
ISBN 13: 978-1-4982-0718-8
Publication date 2/6/2015
Previously published by John Garratt Publishing, 2010

The statue of Lady Justice and the Angel of Mercy
is located outside the Beeson Law Library on the campus of Samford University, Birmingham,
Alabama. "Seek wisdom to temper justice with compassion."
The Angel of Mercy is seen counselling Lady Justice,
staying the sword of justice to keep it from being used too swiftly, tempering it with compassion.
The sculpture is by Glynn Acree.
The digital images in this essay were supplied by Samford University and
are used with permission.

To Mary

*"By the tender mercy of our God, the dawn from on
high will break upon us,
To give light to those who sit in darkness and in the shadow of death,
To guide our feet into the way of peace."*

(Luke 1:78-79)

Acknowledgements

In 2008 and 2009, I gathered at regular intervals with a group of practical theologians in the United States for a research project titled "Catholic Explorations in Practical Theology". This essay owes much to those gatherings and I would like to thank the project coordinators, Dr Kathleen Kahalan (St John's University, Collegeville) and Dr Tom Beaudoin (Fordham University), along with the other members of the research group for their support and feedback.

In October 2009, I had the opportunity to present lectures based on early drafts of this essay at various universities in the United Kingdom. I am especially grateful to my hosts: Dr Elaine Graham at the University of Manchester; Rev Dr James Sweeney at Heythrop College, London; Rev Dr Roger Walton at St John's College, University of Durham; Dr Wayne Morris at the University of Chester; Dr Susan O'Brien at the Margaret Beaufort Institute of Theology, Cambridge University; and Dr Zoe Bennett at the Cambridge Theological Federation. I would also like to thank the Australian Catholic University for making this sabbatical time available to me.

THE BEATITUDE OF MERCY: LOVE WATCHES OVER JUSTICE

✠

CONTENTS

FOREWORD
  By Rev. Michael E. Putney, Bishop of Townsville...........................7

INTRODUCTION 9

CHAPTER ONE – SOCIAL JUSTICE 11
  Justice and Mercy at the Gates of the City 11
  "Before the Law" 14
  The Debt of Justice 18

CHAPTER TWO – SOCIAL MERCY 24
  Mercy Rises above Justice 24
  The Appeal of Mercy 28
  "Mercy Conditions Justice" 33

CHAPTER THREE – SOCIAL HEALING 37
  Beauty and Goodness and "Repairing the World" 37
  Works of Mercy 45
  Social Mercy and the "Little Act of Goodness" 50

ENDNOTES 56

Foreword

In a secular country like Australia, it is difficult to promote Christian beliefs because they often appear so uncongenial to the larger culture. It is easier to promote Christian values because a secular culture can still admire the best of Christian values. The most open of secular commentators would even be prepared to acknowledge the contribution of the teaching of Jesus Christ and of the Christian Tradition to the shaping of some secular values.

Among the values which are espoused as core values for Christians and often the most attractive for those espousing them, and for the larger community, is the value of social justice. It is the value cited most often and most passionately to give credibility to the whole Christian cause in our society.

It is good that social justice has become a central value for contemporary Christians and it is appropriate that it be named as a core value by them. At the same time, social justice, dislocated from its roots in Christian beliefs and the gospel itself, which is not just about our acting justly but also about God's attitude towards us, can sometimes make the cause of social justice a much more political and far less theological value for Christians to espouse. There is a crucial link between what Christians believe and how they live, between theology and social justice.

It is a pity that too often Christians believe they need to shy away from biblical words and biblical concepts in giving an account of the values they espouse. Often the biblical concepts are richer and in fact more fundamental than social justice. One of those words is "charity" which Pope Benedict XVI has explored in two of his three encyclicals.

Another is "mercy" and this book brings it to our attention in a very substantive way.

In some ways one could call this book a "hymn in praise of mercy" but only if one uses the word "hymn" in the great tradition of Protestant hymnology in which the deepest and strongest theological teaching was expounded in the hymns of particular Church communities.

"Mercy" is a richer theological and ethical term than "justice". Without mercy, acting justly and working for social justice can be too limited a cause. Justice finds its best expression within the larger framework and context of mercy, the mercy of God, the mercy we have all received and the mercy we are called to share with others.

It is good that Terry Veling has written about mercy to remind us of this crucial theological context for our Christian vision of social justice. As he wrote:

> If we could be more aware of the need for social mercy, if we could speak more readily of social mercy, if we could let the language and the sentiments of social mercy hold greater sway in our society and our institutions and our social structures, we would in no way jeopardise our quest for social justice. Rather, we would enhance this quest. Mercy is the very foundation of justice, such that without social mercy, our quest for social justice will always be misguided and thwarted.

The very title, *The Beatitude of Mercy: Love Watches over Justice*, situates the two, "mercy" and "justice", in the correct relationship. I am grateful for this small book. It has, as it were, done justice to mercy.

Rev. Michael E. Putney
Bishop of Townsville

Introduction

"Go and learn what this means, 'I desire mercy, not sacrifice'."
Matthew 9:13

What is more important in the world – to act justly, or to act mercifully? Most of us, I suspect, will say that both are equally important. It would be as foolish to renounce justice in the name of mercy, as it would be to renounce mercy in the name of justice. According to St Augustine, we must attend to both:

> Attend to justice and mercy. Do not imagine that these two can be separated in God in any way. They may at first seem to be mutually opposed, so that whoever is merciful would not uphold justice and whoever adheres unconditionally to justice would forget about mercy. But God neither lets go of justice in showing mercy nor of mercy in judging justly.[1]

Maybe a better question to ask is – what is the relationship between justice and mercy? This question is more difficult. Moreover, it is not merely a speculative question. It goes to the heart of many of our activities as human beings in both our personal and social relationships. Am I acting justly toward another? What does it mean to act justly and yet mercifully as well? Are our various social institutions based primarily on fairness and justice, or are they also characterised by love and mercy? Along with our quest for social justice, do we have a similar desire for social mercy? Can we speak of a just person or a just society without, at the same time, speaking of a merciful person and a merciful society?

Questions such as these cannot be answered in any definitive fashion.

Yet they do exercise our mind and our heart; they impinge on our daily lives – in our families, our workplaces, our neighbourhoods, our communities and our society. How can I live with my fellow human beings and God's good creation in ways that are both just and merciful?

The scales of justice and mercy hang precariously. I doubt that the balance between the two is ever perfectly achieved. "Scales", of course, is an image closely associated with the task of justice – fairness, equality, right measure. In the essay that follows, I tilt the scales in favour of mercy. Some may consider this a somewhat unbalanced move on my part, as though I were detracting from justice by writing in favour of mercy. However, if we are going to err in terms of weighing the right measure of justice and mercy, then I think it is better that we err on the side of mercy – if this can be called an "error" at all.

This essay suggests that mercy is not simply a countermeasure or complement to justice; rather, mercy "watches over justice" – not to thwart or deny justice's rightful claims, but to ensure that our practices of justice are never conducted solely according to calculation and measurement, but are also weighed or motivated by mercy and love.

While the language of justice often operates in discursive and rational modes, the language of mercy resists any strict formalisation. It is more poetic in essence and exists in order to persuade, encourage or console its listeners. Human life is often apprehended through intuitive insight and emotional engagement, rather than solely through abstract thinking and impartial appeals to reason.[2] The following work is written in a reflective and existential manner, drawing upon Jewish and Christian sources and written from within the Catholic theological tradition.[3]

✠

CHAPTER ONE – SOCIAL JUSTICE

Justice and Mercy at the Gates of the City

In the late nineties I had a privileged year living in Israel as a Golda Meir Fellow at the Hebrew University of Jerusalem. One of my favourite places to visit was the Mount of Olives with its stunning view over the old city. The walled city of Jerusalem has several large gates that allow access to the city. Yet there is one gate along its eastern wall that remains closed. Known as the "Golden Gate", it has been sealed for hundreds of years, and is one of the oldest and most beautiful gates of the city (referred to in Acts 3:2 as the "Beautiful Gate").

I learnt that this mysterious gate is shrouded in legend and holiness. Unlike the other gates of the city, this one has two large, arched doorways supported by wide columns. According to Jewish tradition, one of the doorways is known as the "Gate of Mercy" and the other as the "Gate of Repentance". Centuries ago, the Jewish people would pray in front of this gate, which faces the Temple area. They would first pray at the Gate of Repentance, and then turn to pray at the Gate of Mercy. According to Christian tradition, Jesus made his last entry into Jerusalem through the Mercy Gate (Matt. 21:1–11). In the Middle Ages, Arabic literature referred to this gate as the gate of Eternal Life.

While the other gates to the city remain open and allow for the comings and goings of people, Jewish tradition holds that this gate will remain closed until the coming of the Messiah, who will enter Jerusalem from the east (Ezek. 44:1–2). It stands as a symbol that the earthly city has not yet achieved the justice and peace of the heavenly city.

Sitting on the Mount of Olives, I often felt pained at the sight of this beautiful and ancient city that is also troubled and torn by conflict. I remembered how Jesus also once wept over the city (Luke 19:41). The beautiful Golden Gate stared back at me, with its sealed archways, a reminder that the troubled ways of humanity have not yet achieved the lasting peace of God. And I thought of the "new Jerusalem", the "holy city", in St John's revelation, "Its gates will never be shut by day – and there will be no night there…God will dwell with them and wipe every tear from their eyes" (Rev. 21:2–4, 25).

The biblical writings contain many references to the gates of the city. The hospitality of the ancient city was extended to the stranger by meeting them at the gate (Gen. 19:1–2). Public markets were typically held at the gate (2 Kings 7:1), as its surrounding spaces were kept wide to allow for the movement and traffic of people, unlike the narrow and winding streets inside the city. The city gate was also the place of justice where the elders sat as a court. "Hate evil and love good, and establish justice at the city gate" (Amos 5:15; see also Job 31:21; Deut. 21:19; 25:17; Prov. 21:23).

Our word for politics is derived from the Greek word for "city" – *polis*. The metaphor of the "city gate" still functions as a striking image for us today. Just as the ancients once gathered at their city gates to conduct public affairs, politics retains this concern for promoting our shared life together. The task of establishing justice and offering hospitality at the gates of our cities (and our nations) remains as vital today as it did in biblical times. "For I know how many are your transgressions," the prophet Amos cries, "and how great are your sins – you who afflict the righteous and push aside the needy at the gate" (Amos 5:12).

In his encyclical, *Octogesima Adveniens: A Call to Action*, Pope Paul VI tells us that we are responsible for the common good and welfare of the city:

> To build up the city, the place where humanity and their expanded communities exist, to create new modes of neighborliness and relationships, to perceive an original application of social justice and to undertake responsibility for this collective future, which is foreseen as difficult, is a task which Christians must share…Let Christians, conscious of this new responsibility, not lose heart in view of the vast and faceless society; let them recall Jonah who traversed Niniveh, the great city, to proclaim therein the good news of God's mercy…In the Bible, the city is often the place of sin and pride – the pride of man who feels secure enough to be able to build his life without God and even to affirm that he is powerful against God. But there is also the example of Jerusalem, the Holy City, the place where God is encountered, the promise of the city which comes from on high.[4]

According to Michael Cowan and Bernard Lee, "God desires a social world characterised by justice and mercy", and the Christian community is "under biblical obligation to order our internal and our public life on behalf of the reign of God in history".[5] They evoke a passage from Jeremiah who speaks of the "well being" or *shalom* of the city: "Seek the well being of the city…for in its well being you will find your well being" (Jer. 29:7). *Shalom* is a word that is rich in biblical meaning. "*Shalom* is the peace which emerges when human beings are in right relationship with themselves, their neighbors, the earth and all its creatures, and God."[6] "For we are members of one another" (Eph. 4:25), St Paul says, and the wellbeing of one affects the wellbeing of all – "if one member suffers, all suffer together with it" (1 Cor. 12:26).

The Beatitude of Mercy: Love Watches over Justice

Humans are primarily social beings, which means we are bound together. Yet while we seek fraternity and friendship, there is a troubling sense in which we live in "gated communities", such that much of our collective existence is marked by what happens at our gates. We do not dwell together in complete openness; rather, we dwell together via a network of doorways that continually open and close. Hardly a day goes by where we do not pass through doors of one kind or another – the doors of our homes, the doors of our offices, the doors of supermarkets, the doors of employment, the doors of airports, the doors of schools and universities, the doors of hospitals and clinics, the doors of churches and temples, the doors of business and government and law – doors that continually open and close in an effort to monitor those who have access and those who are denied. Each of these doorways represents the shalom or wellbeing of the city; they represent the entrance of God's "Peace on Earth", as articulated by Pope John XXIII: access to a dignified life and a worthy standard of living, access to cultural values and the dignity of personhood, access to healthcare and education, to employment and decent working conditions, to freedom of association and freedom of movement, to praise and worship of God, to participation in the city's life and to the common good.[7]

"Before the Law"

It is at the gates of our cities that the task of social justice and the realisation of social good are either served or blocked. In a very telling story titled "Before the Law", Franz Kafka suggests that at every gate there stands a doorkeeper, and that before this gate there is one who seeks permission to enter.

> Before the Law stands a doorkeeper. To this doorkeeper there comes a man from the country who prays for admittance to the Law. But the doorkeeper says he cannot grant admittance at the moment. The man thinks it over and then asks if he will be allowed in later. "It is possible," the doorkeeper says, "but not at the moment." Since the gate stands open, as usual, and the doorkeeper steps to one side, the man

stoops to peer through the gateway into the interior. Observing that, the doorkeeper laughs and says: "If you are so drawn to it, just try to go in despite my veto. But take note: I am powerful. And I am only the least of the doorkeepers. From hall to hall there is one doorkeeper after another, each more powerful than the last…" These are difficulties the man from the country has not expected; the Law, he thinks, should surely be accessible at all times and to everyone…The doorkeeper gives him a stool and lets him sit down at one side of the door. There he sits for days and for years. He makes many attempts to be admitted, and wearies the doorkeeper by his importunity. The doorkeeper frequently has little interviews with him, asking him questions about his home and many other things, but the questions are put indifferently, as great lords put them, and always finish with the statement that he cannot be let in yet…During these many years the man fixes his attention almost continuously on the doorkeeper. He forgets the other doorkeepers, and this first one seems to him the sole obstacle preventing access to the Law. He curses his bad luck, in his early years boldly and loudly; later, as he grows old, he only grumbles to himself. He becomes childish, and since in his yearlong contemplation of the doorkeeper he has come to know even the fleas in his fur collar, he begs the fleas as well to help him and to change the doorkeeper's mind. At length his eyesight begins to fail, and he does not know whether the world is really darker or whether his eyes are only deceiving him. Yet in his darkness he is now aware of a radiance that streams inextinguishably from the gateway of the Law. Now he has not very long to live. Before he dies, all his experiences in these long years gather themselves in his head to one point, a question he has not yet asked the doorkeeper. He waves him nearer, since he can no longer raise his stiffening body. The doorkeeper has to bend low before him, for the difference in height between them has altered much to the man's disadvantage. "What do you want now?" asks the doorkeeper; "you are insatiable." "Everyone strives to reach the Law," says the man, "so how does it happen that for all these many years no one but myself has begged for admittance?" The doorkeeper recognizes that the man has reached his end, and, to let his failing senses catch the words, roars in his ear: "No one else could ever be admitted here, since this gate was made only for you. I am now going to shut it."[8]

The man in Kafka's story "prays for admittance to the Law". The Law, presumably, represents access to justice and "should be accessible at all times to everyone". While the gate to the Law stands open, the gatekeeper is powerful and refuses entrance. The man has a chance to peer inside. "From hall to hall there is one doorkeeper after another, each more powerful than the last." So the man sits "for days and years" and he begs even the fleas to help him gain admittance. He grows old and frail and the world grows darker, yet a radiance continues to shine from the gateway of the Law. Justice shines brightly as "everyone strives to reach the Law". The man wonders why no one else is seeking admittance, and the doorkeeper roars in his ear, "this gate was made only for you" – and then he shuts the gate.

The Law, which serves justice, is meant for everyone. It is meant to radiate its light for the good of all – a justice that is a *social justice* that serves the common good. Yet Kafka suggests that the Law must deal with each singular person – case by case – and in this sense the gate of the Law is not simply for everyone, but for each and every particular person – "for you alone". The Law is of no use to "everyone" unless it can be of particular use to *someone*. The Law's universal reach often fails to reach each and every person who seeks access to justice. In this sense, whenever there is one who has been denied access to the Law, then the Law has failed to serve justice's universal claims.

There are many who stand at the gate, many who seek admittance, and many who spend even their entire lives seeking entrance to the gateways that characterise the *polis,* yet whose access is often blocked by powerful gatekeepers. It is to the guardians of the Law that Jesus says: "You shut up the kingdom of heaven in men's faces, neither going in yourselves nor allowing others to go in who want to" (Matt. 23:13). Many of Jesus' parables and many of his actions were concerned with defending those whose access to justice was denied, those who were left standing outside the gates of the Law, those who were cast off from the promises of God's kingdom – the excluded, the accused, the debarred, the victims, the least, the poor, the disadvantaged. It is for these that the Law exists – "the Sabbath was made for humankind" (Mark 2:27) – and yet it is often these whom the Law leaves waiting and languishing at its gates. Instead of being the "preferred ones" before the Law – the ones whose claims are most urgent, the ones who suffer injustice and a lack of wellbeing – they are too often treated as "the least" before the Law. In the kingdom of heaven, however, it is these "least" and "last" who are of special concern to God, who receive the "preferential love of God". As Jesus says on another occasion to the gatekeepers of the Law, "the tax-collectors and the prostitutes are going into the kingdom of God ahead of you" (Matt. 21:31).

God's "preferential option for the poor" challenges our notion of the Law's presumed impartiality and equality, often symbolised as a blindfolded woman ("Lady Justice") who sees no distinctions between people, and who holds a set of scales that balances everything with perfect equilibrium. By contrast, the biblical kingdom favours the poor and criticises the rich, which is a great joy to Jesus' mother, Mary. "My soul magnifies the Lord," she sings, "for he has scattered the proud in the thoughts of their hearts. He has brought down the powerful from their thrones, and lifted up the lowly; he has filled the hungry with good things and sent the rich away empty" (Luke 1:51–54).

The United States' Catholic Bishops note that the option for the poor is "a call to have a special openness with the small and the weak, those that suffer and weep, those that are humiliated and left on the margin of society, so as to help them win their dignity as human persons and children of God".[9] They go on to say that the option for the poor is not a pitting of one group over another; rather, "it states that the deprivation and powerlessness of the poor wounds the whole community. The extent of their suffering is the measure of how far we are from being a true community of persons".[10]

The poor are always in our midst. They are not only the "economically poor", but all those "who cannot cope" and who find themselves suddenly burdened or stricken for one reason or another – the unemployed worker, the single parent, the illegal immigrant, those overwhelmed by debt, or evicted by the landlord, or arrested on the streets. It is these who are members of the *polis* – who stand at our city gates, seeking justice – and yet who are often most ignored. According to Gustavo Gutiérrez, "the poor are non-persons, the *in-significant*, those who do not count in society and all too often in Christian churches as well". He goes on to say: "We do not know the names of the poor; they are anonymous and remain so. They are insignificant in society *but not before God*."[11]

For the biblical prophets, the gates of heaven can never be closed to the gates of the city. God tells Jeremiah to "stand at the gate of the Lord's house, and proclaim there this word…You that enter these gates to worship the Lord…Amend your ways and your doings, and let me dwell with you in this place…If you do not oppress the alien, the orphan, and the widow…then I will dwell with you in this place" (Jer. 7:2–7). Commenting on this passage, Gutiérrez notes that Jeremiah "makes it perfectly clear that until there is a commitment to the rights of the poor, God will not dwell with them in the temple; God is absent because the people do not practice justice, especially towards the weakest among them".[12]

There are many who do not count "before the Law", but they do count "before God". If there are any among us who find ourselves serving as gatekeepers of the Law, then our task is to help those who come before us to gain access to justice – to life and liberty and wellbeing, to the *shalom* of the city. If we are teachers, if we are pastors, if we are health care workers, if we are lawyers, if we are in positions of authority, if we are business leaders, if we are shopkeepers, if we are police officers, if we are public servants, if we are parents or neighbours or citizens – if we are members of one another – then we need to ensure that everyone who comes our way is enabled to have access to dignity and justice in all the gates of our city.

The Debt of Justice

Justice is a debt that we owe to those who have been denied the wellbeing of human flourishing. Justice is "being-enjoined" to each other, beholden to each other.[13] Wherever we find people who lack basic social goods that are rooted in their very dignity as human persons, then justice is *owing*. Justice serves the common good and not simply the good of a few. St John Chrysostom writes: "Not to enable the poor to share in our goods is to steal from them and deprive them of life. The goods we possess are not ours, but theirs."[14] The beggar on the backstreets is not asking for a handout; the beggar is asking why we have stolen so much. When we attend to those who are in need, we are not giving them what is ours; rather, we are giving them what is theirs – "we are paying a debt of justice".[15]

Justice is what we *owe* and places us in debt, though it is not uncommon to hear people saying that the beggar on the street has already received their just deserts, that they are on the street because of a fault that they bear, and that should we decide to give them anything, then we consider it an act of charity – giving them something that belongs to us – rather than a debt of justice, giving them something that belongs to them.

We do not typically feel in debt to the beggar or to those who, like the blind man in the Gospel of Mark, cry out for mercy (Mark 10:46–52). And yet in his encyclical *Sollicitudo Rei Socialis: On Social Concern* Pope John Paul II notes that "at stake is the *dignity of the human person*, whose *defense and promotion* have been entrusted to us by the Creator, and to whom the men and women at every moment in history are strictly and responsibly *in debt*".[16] In one of Jesus' most haunting parables, we find ourselves face-to-face with this debt. "There was a rich man who was dressed in purple and fine linen and who feasted sumptuously every day. And at his gate lay a poor man named Lazarus, covered with sores, who longed to satisfy his hunger with what fell from the rich man's table…" (Luke 16:19–21). The poor man dies and is carried away by angels to be with Abraham. The rich man dies and is sent to Hades where he is tormented by scorching flames. The rich man begs Abraham for mercy. But Abraham replies, "Child, remember that during your lifetime you received your good things, and Lazarus in like manner evil things; but now he is comforted here, and you are in agony" (v. 25). Justice is served. The debt is paid. Here we are face to face with the debt of justice pure and simple, exacting and unrelenting: once you were rich and comfortable, now you are in agony. Once you neglected the cries of the suffering; now your own cries are neglected. Moreover, the severity of justice is such that "a great chasm has been fixed" so that none can cross from the fires of justice into the balm of mercy. It is a terrifying scene, repeated in the

The Beatitude of Mercy: Love Watches over Justice

Letter of St James (5:1–5):

> Come now, you rich people, weep and wail for the miseries that are coming to you. Your riches have rotted, and your clothes are moth-eaten. Your gold and silver have rusted, and their rust will be evidence against you, and it will eat your flesh like fire. Listen! The wages of the labourers who mowed your fields, which you kept back by fraud, cry out, and the cries of the harvesters have reached the ears of the Lord of hosts. You have lived on earth in luxury and pleasure; you have fattened your hearts in a day of slaughter.

The prophet Amos warns us not to be too quick to long for the day of justice. "Alas for you who desire the day of the Lord! Why do you want the day of the Lord? It is darkness, not light; as if someone fled from a lion, and was met by a bear; or went into the house…and was bitten by a snake. Is not the day of the Lord darkness, not light, and gloom with no brightness in it?" (Amos 5:18–20).

We should be wary of evoking the word "justice" too readily, especially when we consider Jesus' words, "Let anyone among you who is without sin be the first to throw a stone…" (John 8:7). "It might seem strange to say this," writes Gutiérrez, "but *justice can become an idol*."[17] We can all too easily think that we are acting justly, that our laws are just, that our society is just, that the guilty are rightfully judged, the poor are taken care of, and the accused are justly locked away. We can turn justice into an idol, bowing to the civilised rule of law, trumpeting our own righteousness, parading our supposed freedom and democracy for all to see and admire. "God, I thank you that I am not like the other people" (Luke 18:11). If we have this attitude, Jesus says, we will not find favour in God's sight, but if we pray "God, be merciful to me, a sinner", God will look with favour upon us.

Pope John Paul II notes that "human action can deviate from justice itself, even when it is being undertaken in the name of justice".[18] We can easily deceive ourselves into thinking that we are acting justly and, for this reason, John Paul II suggests that without mercy, justice cannot be established. "The experience of the past and of our own time demonstrates that justice alone is not enough, that it can even lead to the negation of itself, if *that deeper power, which is love*, is not allowed to shape human life in its various dimensions."[19] The pope refers to the ancient saying, attributed to Cicero, *summum ius, summa iniuria*, which can be translated as "the more justice, the more injury" or "the extreme law is the greatest injustice".[20] Justice requires mercy to ensure that our practices of judgement and justice are not harsh or severe, so that we can act *humanely* with tolerance and restraint, "bearing with one another in love" (Eph. 4:2). The pope writes:

> Society can become ever more human only if we introduce into the many-sided setting of interpersonal and social relationships, not merely justice, but also that "merciful love" which constitutes the messianic message of the Gospel…A world from which forgiveness was eliminated would be nothing but a world of cold and unfeeling justice, in the name of which each person would claim his or her own rights vis-à-vis others; the various kinds of selfishness latent in man would transform life and human society into an arena of permanent strife between one group and another.[21]

According to Simone Weil, this "cold and unfeeling justice" is often narrowly associated with the language of rights. Whenever someone cries "Why am I being hurt?" then we are in the realm of evil and injustice. This is in contrast, Weil suggests, to another cry that is all too commonly heard: "Why has somebody else got more than I have?"[22] This is the "cry of rights", of which she says:

> The notion of rights is linked with the notion of sharing out, of exchange, of measured quantity. It has a commercial flavor, essentially evocative of legal claims and arguments. Rights are always asserted in a tone of contention; and when this tone is adopted, it must rely upon force…[23]

There is a latent violence associated with the language of rights, especially when these are asserted in a narrowly self-interested manner of "what is owed to me". Weil writes:

> Every time we put forth some effort and the equivalent of this effort does not come back to us in the form of some visible fruit, we have a sense of false balance which makes us think that we have been cheated. The effort of suffering from some offence causes us to expect the punishment or apologies of the offender, the effort of doing good makes us expect the gratitude of the person we have helped…Every time we give anything out we have an absolute need that at least the equivalent should come back to us, and because we need this we think we have a right to it. Our debtors comprise all beings and all things; they are the entire universe. We think we have claims everywhere.[24]

Many of Jesus' parables are scandalous and irritating because they offend our human sense of justice as fairness, equality and rights. "For the kingdom of heaven is like a landowner who went out early in the morning to hire labourers for his vineyard. After agreeing with the labourers for the usual daily wage, he sent them into the vineyard" (Matt. 20:1–2). That seems fair and just. Yet the story continues. Toward the end of the day, the landowner sees some workers who have not been hired, and so he says, "You also go into the vineyard." The workers are then called to receive their wages. Those who came first, and spent a whole day working in the field, receive the same wages as those who came last and spent only an hour working in the field. The workers who came first are scandalised at the injustice of it all, saying, "These last worked only one hour, and you have made them equal to us who have borne the burden of the day and the scorching heat" (v. 12). The landowner replies that he has paid them what they agreed to, and that surely he can be generous to the other workers if it pleases him. Our notions of equality and justice are often offended by acts of generosity. The parable of the prodigal son and the disgruntled brother (Luke 15:11–32) makes a similar point – God is gracious and "rich in mercy" (Eph. 2:4).

Perhaps the most telling parable concerning the relationship between justice and mercy is the parable of the unmerciful servant (Matt. 18:23–35). In this parable, the kingdom of heaven is like a king who is collecting debts from his servants. One of the servants owes him ten thousand talents (an enormous debt for those times). The servant cannot pay and so the king orders that the servant, his wife, his children and all his possessions be sold. The servant falls to his knees and pleads for mercy, and out of pity for him, the king releases him and forgives all his debt. The servant then meets someone who owes him a small amount and demands that just repayment be made. His fellow servants are scandalised that he is demanding justice after having himself received mercy. They report his actions to the king who decides that the servant will now be subjected to the demands of justice, handing him over to be tortured until he pays his entire debt. Jesus concludes the parable with these haunting words: "So my heavenly Father will also do to every one of you, if you do not forgive your brother or sister from your heart" (v. 35). This is a statement of justice, yet it is based or founded upon justice's highest requirement: to be merciful.

✜

CHAPTER TWO – SOCIAL MERCY

Mercy Rises above Justice

I recently spent a few evenings searching the indexes of my books, looking for entries on "mercy". I was surprised at the paucity of references, though when I looked up "justice", entries abounded. It seems that mercy is a rather silent word and perhaps – of its nature – does not draw attention to itself. Mercy is a special type of love. "It is not boastful or conceited," St Paul says. It is not "jealous". It does not "take pleasure in other people's sins". It is "always ready to excuse" (1 Cor. 13:4–7). Mercy sits among the "least" and the "last", hidden and unknown by the powers-that-be. Mercy never forces its way to gain attention, but always remains *there* nevertheless, full of import for every soul who knows that, in the end, they have little else they can rely on;

there is little else that will save either their own or *our* situation – in this sense, mercy is "from age to age" (Luke 1:50). It has the greatest import for every *living* soul – if, that is, they are living and in this sense, *soulful* and *merciful*.

When I think about social mercy – the need for it, the lack of it, the fragility of it – I feel an enormous pain or ache in my heart. On one particular occasion, I witnessed a heart-wrenching act of injustice. However, I found myself asking: "Why do I perceive this as an unmerciful act, much more so than as an act of injustice?"

It is difficult to write in the name of mercy. It is also difficult, though I think less so, to write in the name of justice. Many do, and often. From water-cooler conversations in the workplace, to political platforms, to newspaper commentaries, to advocates and campaigners, to religious groups – the concerns of justice are readily (and sometimes) rightly invoked. Most people like to think that they are concerned for social justice in our world. I don't think I've yet read an institutional mission statement that doesn't say somewhere "and we are committed to social justice" or some such declaration.

Like most people, I too am concerned for justice. I feel it as a duty or an obligation. I feel it in the lives of those who have suffered hardship and too many blows – people who suffer from inequitable or discriminatory structures, people who are disadvantaged, who bear a heavy burden, who are denied basic human goods – work, health care, a home, refuge, a measure of wellbeing and happiness. As Simone Weil notes, "Every time there arises from the depths of a human heart the cry which Christ himself could not restrain, 'Why am I being hurt?', then there is certainly injustice."[25] It is incumbent upon me and all of us – as a society, as humans who are bound together – to work for social justice, and to never tire of this responsibility and obligation toward our brother and sister in need.

And yet. And yet? Surely there is no "and yet" that can be said in the wake of justice's demands. Isn't justice incontestable?

Isn't it a requirement that binds us all – a requirement that every public discourse and religious tradition worth its salt urges us to seek and to do? Yes, indeed. We cannot shy from this. And yet, I can't help asking myself – what of mercy? Who speaks of mercy? Where does mercy come into play? Could we, for example, speak as readily in our various civic and religious discourses about "social mercy" as we do about "social justice"? I wonder whether anyone could really understand if we began advocating for, speaking of, placing in our "mission statements", or utilising as our "platform" the notion of social mercy. What sort of statements would we make, or what type of policies would we devise, or what kind of actions would we promote, if we were to speak of "social mercy" as resolutely as we speak of "social justice"?

There is much that is unjust in our society, yet I have often wondered whether it is the lack of mercy that causes injustice to prevail. Or rather, that without mercy, justice is perilously close to becoming unjust. This had led me to believe that mercy is not the opposite of justice – or the complement of justice – but its very condition.

French philosopher Jacques Derrida, famously known for the word "deconstruction", had a longstanding interest in questions concerning justice. In a celebrated essay he makes the bold claim that "justice in itself, if such a thing exists, outside or beyond the law, is not deconstructible".[26] Derrida draws a distinction between justice and "the law". By "law" he means all the legal systems, codes, rights, and institutions that exist in an effort to ensure that the claims of justice are met. The law exists for the sake of justice and yet "justice in itself" is never fully realised. Because of this, the law must be continually deconstructed – critiqued, revised, reformed – so that it can better approximate the justice that it seeks, yet always falls short of. If laws were not "deconstructible", we would end up in a fixed system and any hope of achieving justice would be lost to us. However, it is "justice in itself" that prompts the revision and critique of the law, that prevents the law from thinking that it is *in itself* "undeconstructible", that it is *in itself* justice – whereas the law is only a means to justice, which always stands "outside or beyond the law" as the undeconstructible "test" of the law. In a round-table discussion, Derrida makes his case this way:

> There is a history of legal systems, of rights, of laws, and this history is the history of the transformation of laws. You can improve the law, you can replace one law by another one…So, the law as such can be deconstructed and has to be deconstructed. That is the condition of historicity, revolution, morals, ethics, and progress. But justice is not the law. Justice is what gives the impulse, the drive, or the movement to improve the law, that is, to deconstruct the law. Without a call for justice we would not have any interest in deconstructing the law… Deconstruction is a call for justice. Justice is not reducible to the law, to a given system of legal structures…That is why the call for justice is never, never fully answered. That is why no one can say "I am just."[27]

Derrida establishes justice – or the call of justice – as that which forever prevents our laws and moral codes from thinking that they in themselves are "just" or that they in themselves are equal to "justice".[28] This strikes me as a persuasive argument – and yet – I find myself wondering whether it is justice alone that is "beyond the law" and undeconstructible, or whether it is mercy that rises even higher than justice as that which cannot be deconstructed. My own sense is that *mercy* remains as the everlasting appeal that keeps even justice itself from becoming the final arbiter or test of our laws and our moral codes. The call of justice always contains within itself an appeal for mercy. When we seek to be just, it is not only justice that we seek, it is also mercy. Without mercy, *even justice itself* cannot save us.

Perhaps it is because no one can say "I am just" that the call of mercy rises above justice as the highest appeal. For if no one can claim to be just, then each of us will be continually dependent on mercy's appeal ("forgive us our debts, as we forgive those who are in debt to us" – Matt. 6:12). Mercy stands "outside or beyond the law" as the ultimate appeal that keeps even *justice itself* answerable to a higher call – the call of mercy.

The Appeal of Mercy

"I know that I'm forgiven, but I don't know how I know," the poet Leonard Cohen says.[29] How do we learn to dwell mercifully in the world? How can we even speak of mercy, or even know of its existence?

To dwell mercifully in the world is not to say "I will be merciful". It is to be aware that we are recipients rather than masters or dispensers of mercy.[30] To dwell mercifully in the world is to know that mercy has been shown to me, that I have received mercy, that my existence is all the time supported and upheld by mercy. We can speak of mercy only as we receive it, only as it has been shown to us.

Danish ethicist Knud Løgstrup writes: "To decide to show trust or mercifulness is to decide to surrender oneself to trust and mercy. Trust and mercifulness must be there already as life-possibilities. If they are not, no decision can elicit them."[31] This is why Løgstrup calls mercy a *sovereign expression of life*. It is a sovereign expression of life because "there is nothing antecedent to mercy that might move it, nor is there anything beyond mercy that might relativise it or escape from it".[32] And yet, we embark upon strange manoeuvres in the name of justice, for adjudicating evils and setting things right, such as just wars and just causes and just outcomes. Justice, however, is always tied to mercy's appeal. Jon Sobrino writes:

> Mercy is a basic attitude toward the suffering of another, whereby one responds to eradicate that suffering for the sole reason that it exists, and in the conviction that, in this response to the ought-not-to-be of another's suffering, one's own being, without any possibility of subterfuge, hangs in the balance.[33]

Mercy is not simply one phenomenon in human reality among many. Not only is mercy "the greatest of the attributes and perfections attributable to God",[34] and not only is mercy the highest principle in the life of Jesus and the gospels, mercy also "directly defines the human being".[35] To be a human being is to respond with mercy. "Without this response," Sobrino writes, "the essence of the human is vitiated in its root, as occurred with the priest and the Levite who 'saw him and went on'…When the priest and the Levite show no mercy, Jesus is horrified."[36]

Among all the appeals that strike the ears and the hearts of human beings, mercy is the highest and everywhere the first. It is the appeal of the suffering one. It is the appeal of God. Mercy beckons us, in the very first instance and at every turn, and then finally in the end, as the one hope of humanity. Løgstrup writes:

> Mercifulness is elicited by the perception of another person being hampered in the realization of their life. It appeals to as elemental a hope as that of seeing every life realized. The other person's lot is at odds with that hope, and from the dissonance inherent in that circumstance is born mercifulness that seeks, through action, to vindicate the hope and remove what stands in the way of its fulfillment – whether the obstacles be poverty, need, oppression, or exploitation.[37]

Mercy is a rich and deeply layered word. Canadian theologian Heather Chappell draws out the following qualities:

> *Mercy towards the suffering:* an affective response that seeks to actively relieve someone's distress; a charity influenced by a softening or a change of mind and heart; an inclining of the heart toward another; compassion toward another's pain.
>
> *Mercy towards sin:* forgiveness and clemency; the gift of release, yielding, staying the hand against someone; a letting go, a setting free.
>
> *Mercy as a surprise blessing:* unexpected leniency; the gift of tolerance, forbearance, restraint, moderation, mildness; a disposition against all strictness and severity; a kindly refraining from the infliction of punishment or pain; a blessing regarded as an act of divine favour or compassion.[38]

The Beatitude of Mercy: Love Watches over Justice

Pope John Paul II notes that sometimes mercy is dubiously presented as a relationship of inequality between the one who offers mercy and the one who receives it, such that mercy belittles or humiliates the receiver. However, "mercy is manifested in its true and proper aspect when it restores to value, promotes and *draws good from all the forms of evil* existing in the world and in the person".[39] Mercy does not diminish human value and dignity; rather, it acts to restore the dignity that is proper to human life. "In reciprocal relationships between persons, merciful love is never a unilateral act or process…An act of merciful love is only really such when we are *deeply convinced*…that we are at the same time *receiving* mercy from the people who are accepting it from us."[40]

Mercy is not simply something that we "feel" or "offer" to another. Rather, as Chappell notes, "mercy *requires something of us*: that we relent, that we change our mind and heart, that we give up a previous understanding of another, that we release them from the bondage of our preconception, and finally that we stoop down and bear with them in their suffering."[41] Mercy therefore contains within itself the movement of repentance, conversion, or *metanoia*. "Be merciful, just as your Father is merciful" (Luke 6:36).

If we know that we are sinful human beings who often err and go astray, and yet God has dealt mercifully with us, then we should deal mercifully with others. If we know that we are forgiven, and have experienced God's "amazing grace", then we should be no less amazing in our actions toward one another. If we have felt the generosity of God's love, and we truly believe in the "glad tidings" of the Gospel, then our lives should also be good news for others. Edward Schillebeeckx writes:

> God's merciful dealing – demonstrated clearly in Jesus' own compassion for people – must be exemplary for anyone who wishes to enter the kingdom of God…For since God's lordship is the universal, compassionate disposition of God towards humanity, the *metanoia* demanded by the kingdom takes concrete form in empathy with and dedicated commitment to one's fellow human beings.[42]

Mercy and *metanoia* are intimately linked. It is because we know the "gate of mercy" that we are able to pray at "the gate of repentance". Without the offer of mercy, repentance would be futile. To confess our sin, to change our ways, to repent of our wrongdoing, to turn to our neighbour with compassion is only possible if we know that mercy, rather than condemnation, awaits us at the gate of repentance. We are all guilty, and we are all the time bearing each other's faults. We are all trespassers before God and before each other, and without mercy there would be no hope for any of us. It is only within the context of mercy that deep and practical *metanoia* is possible. As Chappell notes, "In all conversions from suffering to hope, from sin to release, and from despair to faith, mercy is the effective element which offers a future and enables change."[43] Only mercy can transform "hearts of stone" into "hearts of flesh" (Ezek. 36:26).

There is an interesting Talmudic text that says God created seven things before the creation of the world. Repentance (*teshuvah*) is one of the seven entities *created before the world itself*.[44] "The implication of this remarkable statement," writes Rabbi Adin Steinsaltz, "is that repentance is a universal, primordial phenomenon."[45] Even before the first human person was created, God provided a way for humanity to amend the course of their life, to turn away from sin and to return to God. Even though the events of the past are "fixed", repentance allows for the possibility of changing the consequence and significance of past events – and therefore, of time itself. This is why repentance is referred to as something created before the world and before time. God recognised that the world could not exist or sustain itself without the prior creation of repentance – because repentance creates the possibility for renewed existence and new futures.

Jewish philosopher Hannah Arendt ties the act of repentance and forgiveness directly to the act of promising and creation. Human action that is life-giving shares in the creative action of God, who is continually bringing forth and sustaining life and existence. Every act that serves life is an act of "bringing forth", of pledging oneself to the coming of something new, to the promise of new life:

> Without action, without the capacity to start something new and thus articulate the new beginning that comes into the world with the birth of each human being, the life of man, spent between birth and death, would indeed be doomed beyond salvation…Action, with all its uncertainties, is like an ever-present reminder that men, though they must die, are not born in order to die but in order to begin something new. *Initium ut esset homo creatus est* – "that there be a beginning man was created," said Augustine. With the creation of man, the principle of beginning came into the world…[46]

"I promise, I am here *for you*" is one of our most fundamental human acts. "Binding ourselves through promises," says Arendt, is the only way we can sustain our life together. "Without being bound to the fulfillment of promises, each of us would be condemned helplessly and without direction in the darkness of his own lonely heart."[47] The act of promising invests the future with hope. Promising looks forward as a commitment to the future and to each other.

Arendt knows, however, that we live in a world of broken promises, that our social and interpersonal relationships are wounded and frail and in need of healing and repair. For this reason, she suggests that acts of promising must also be accompanied by acts of repentance and forgiveness.

Promising and forgiving belong together, go hand-in-hand, because we often fail in our promises, and forgiveness allows us to begin again, to renew the covenantal relations between us. "Without being forgiven," writes Arendt, without being "released from the consequences of what we have done, our capacity to act would, as it were, be confined to one single deed from which we could never recover; we would remain the victims of its consequences forever…"[48]

To promise and to forgive are the threads that keep us woven and bound to each other. We need to keep promising, over and over again. And because we know our human frailty, we also need to keep forgiving, over and over again. "How often should I forgive?" Peter asks Jesus, "As many as seven times?" "Not seven times," Jesus replies, "but seventy-seven times" (Matt. 18:21–22). In other words, all the time, because we are constantly failing each other.

Trespassing is a daily occurrence in life that needs acts of forgiveness in order to make it possible for the promise of life to go on. Rather than clinging tight to past hurts and injuries, forgiveness offers us the promise of a new future, a new beginning. Forgiveness sets us free from the burden of sin and starts up a new chain of events. "Go, and sin no more" (John 8:11). By constantly releasing us from the burden of what we have done to one another, acts of forgiveness break the cycles of violence and vengeance, of death and destruction. Only in this way can we "choose life" rather than always "keeping score".[49]

"Mercy Conditions Justice"

There is an intriguing passage in the Talmud that talks about God praying. The rabbis ask: What does God pray for? "May it be My will that My mercy may suppress My anger, and that My mercy may prevail over My other attributes, so that I may deal with My children in the attribute of mercy and, on their behalf, stop short of the limit of strict justice."[50]

The Jewish tradition is exemplary in illustrating that mercy, rather than justice, remains as the great undeconstructible "name of God". God's faithfulness is always demonstrated, not in strict justice, but in mercy (*rahamim*). God is always "mindful of his mercy" (Luke 1:54) before he is mindful of his justice. Or rather, and even more radically, God cannot act "justly" except that he acts mercifully – with tenderness and love.[51] If God were not merciful, God would not be just. As we see in the following passage, when the Israelites appeal to God, they appeal to God's justice because they know that they cannot rely on their own "justice" or "good works". However, when they appeal to God's justice, they are asking God to act "for God's own sake", according to God's own name. They are asking God to be responsible for his own love, to be faithful to his own love, to be just according to himself – to act according to the mercy that bears his name.

> Lord, by all your acts of justice turn away your anger from Jerusalem, your own city... Listen to the prayer and pleading of your servant. For your own sake, Lord, let your face smile again on your desolate sanctuary. Listen, my God, listen to us; open your eyes and look on our plight and on the city that bears your name. We are not relying on our own good works but on your great mercy, to commend our humble appeal to you. Listen, Lord! Lord, forgive! Hear, Lord and act! For your own sake, my God, do not delay, because they bear your name, this is your city, this is your people (Daniel 9:16–19).

In the early eighties Poland was torn by conflict and violence. Polish composer Henryk Górecki responded to the tragic events with his symphony for voice titled *Miserere*.[52] Its unaccompanied form consists of a text of only five words – "Domine Deus noster, Miserere nobis" – "Lord our God, have mercy on us". Over an extraordinarily beautiful and sustained span of some twenty-five minutes, the voices rise and fall with their plaintive and lamenting appeal – "Domine Deus noster". These three words fill the main body of the work, repeated over and over again in waves of choral voice – "Domine Deus noster" – "Lord, our God", "Lord our God", "Lord our God". The final words, "Miserere nobis" ("Have mercy on us"), are saved until the concluding three minutes. It is as if Górecki senses the long, suffering cries of the human heart, pleading to God in the midst of so much heedless violence and human hatred, only to finally surrender in the last moments to the mercy of God. "Something of a sigh of mercy, of compassion, is hidden in the deepest depths of reality," writes Schillebeeckx, "and in it believers hear the name of God."[53]

I have a portrait in my home of St Vincent de Paul meeting Christ the beggar. They meet on the road, and it happens that St Vincent has just returned from the village store and is holding a loaf of bread. He breaks a piece of bread and hands it to Christ the beggar. Christ receives it, and their hands meet, with both hands in a posture of openness (the sort of humble and unbounded openness that is required for all giving and receiving). Their simple clothing – the cloak of a beggar and the cloak of a monk, and their furrowed and worn faces – suggest that that they are both poor. Their eyes are locked in a gaze of mutually recognised pain and compassion – each for the other. Their bodies are both bowed down, suggesting either the shared weight of their poverty – their shared circumstance – or maybe the reverence in which they behold each other.

The beggar is perhaps one of our most ancient symbols of the supplicant – the one who pleads for mercy – symbol of Christ, symbol of humanity, symbol of each one of us. Speaking of the poet who recognises this, Charles Péguy writes: "One thing we may be sure of, when the poet sees a beggar by the road, he sees him the way he really is, really sees him the way he really is…sees him, the ancient beggar, the ancient supplicant, on the ancient road."[54]

In a strange and maybe mystical statement, Pope John Paul II notes that "in a special way, God reveals his mercy when he *invites man to have 'mercy' on his only Son, the Crucified One*".[55] When we show mercy to each other, "Christ accepts it as if it were shown to himself".[56] In the end, the merciful do not obtain justice. Rather, they obtain mercy. "Blessed are the merciful…for they shall obtain mercy" (Matt. 5:7). This is mercy's strange "logic" or strange "justice" – only the merciful shall attain mercy. Thus, even justice itself begins and ends in mercy. This is the Beatitude of Mercy.

"*Mercy differs from justice,*" Pope John Paul II says, "*but is not in opposition to it.*" Rather, "mercy conditions justice" in the sense that mercy is primary and fundamental; mercy reveals the perfection of justice; mercy is "a mark of the whole of revelation".[57] Indeed, "*true mercy is the most profound source of justice*".[58] The pope writes:

> Mercy is an indispensable element for *shaping* mutual relationships between people…It is impossible to establish this bond between people, if they wish to regulate their mutual relationships solely according to the measure of justice. In every sphere of interpersonal relationships justice must, so to speak, *be 'corrected' to a considerable extent*…by that *merciful love* which is so much of the essence of the Gospel and Christianity.[59]

This is not an escape from the demands of justice. Rather, this is a heightening of justice's concerns to the very pinnacle where we recognise that only mercy can ultimately perfect the justice that we seek. Mercy is love. Mercy is compassion. Mercy is solidarity. Mercy is at the heart of God. Mercy is good news for justice, not bad news.

✠

CHAPTER THREE – SOCIAL HEALING

Beauty and Goodness and "Repairing the World"

In the Jewish mystical tradition, the Kabbalah, the world exists because mercy (*Hesed*) and justice (*Din*) are in balance. *Hesed* represents God's abundant goodness and loving light. It is the "vessel" or means through which "God's unrestrained love flows down into the lower regions, a source of the purest blessing and goodness".[60] Mercy is counterbalanced by *Din* (justice). Justice is a limit on excessive love, which can be too blinding or overwhelming for humans to bear. Justice limits and proportions "what is due" in fairness and equal measure, which is an easier thing for humans to accept. However, in the Kabbalistic tradition, while *Din* is necessary for all existence, it is also regarded as the root of evil. "*Din* is capable of becoming fully-fledged evil when it fails to remain in harmonious balance with *Hesed*."[61] This is especially true because of the propensity of human sinfulness. If our struggle for justice is divorced from God's overflowing love, we are in danger of inflicting further damage, as is suggested in the following maxim: "The fiercer the struggle against the injustice you suffer, the blinder you will be to the injustice you inflict."[62] In other words, we can often turn the presumed transgression of our "enemies" into an arena for our own righteousness. Jesus' parable about removing the splinter in your neighbour's eye while not recognising the log in your own is a prime example of this (Matt. 7:3–5).

In the Kabbalah, the harmonising principle between mercy and justice is beauty (*Tiferet*). When the right balance of justice and mercy is achieved, the result is beauty – the world is restored to its original goodness and is refashioned in the image of divine loveliness. Beauty is the "offspring" of mercy and justice – indeed, Beauty is their "Son" – "The Holy One, Blessed Be He".[63] It seems that the relationship between justice and mercy cannot be resolved or balanced without the mediating principle of "beauty", or what is known in the Christian tradition as the "beatitude of God". "Everything which originates from pure love," writes Simone Weil, "is lit with the radiance of beauty."[64]

In his reflections on justice and mercy, St Thomas Aquinas says that justice is primarily concerned with *suum cuique* – "to each what is due" – such that justice is primarily about fairness and the just distribution of society's goods.[65] However, "to each what is due" is a rather narrow conception. Aquinas goes on to say that justice needs to be situated within the larger confidence of God's original goodness – a goodness that inspires a shared love, and not simply "what is due". This covenantal love is the very basis of the "common good", which is a key theme of Catholic social teaching. Justice always has as its "end" or "form" the original goodness of divine creation, which is the very basis of justice, the condition of its possibility.[66] "Without this orientation toward a shared love," writes Daniel Bell, "justice becomes a shadow of its former self, content to function simply as a procedural power of distribution and exchange."[67]

The beatitude of divine goodness suggests that God's mercy is the fullness of God's justice, for God does more than simply what is required or what is due. Rather, God's mercy is full of grace that desires all to share in divine life. According to Aquinas:

> The work of divine justice always presupposes the work of mercy; and is founded thereupon…God acts mercifully, not indeed by going against justice, but by doing something more than justice…Mercy does not destroy justice, but is the fullness thereof. And thus it is said: *Mercy exalteth itself above judgement* (James 2:13).[68]

Aquinas is articulating a deeply held Catholic position that affirms the goodness and graciousness of all creation. This is the way of the analogical imagination (the *analogia entis*), which sees everything in creation as lovingly crafted in God's image. This instinct or aspiration toward beauty and goodness draws us to consider the world as a "correspondence of heaven" or an "analogy of heaven". Those who achieve this poetic vision are those who live on earth "as if" they were living in heaven, as if everything was alive in God – even those who have died, even the sinner. The mystical or analogical imagination does not pull me out of this world to some other world; rather, it changes what it means to be in this world.

The analogical imagination perceives that a moral and vital "law of life" pervades the universe and it is the human vocation to align their lives with this creative goodness. It is a profound affirmation, a yes to life and to the holiness of life. In the mystical tradition this is known as the experience of *kataphasis* – affirmation, wonder, giving thanks, and "speaking-with" rather than against life's goodness and beauty. As Gustavo Gutiérrez notes, "the gratuitousness of God's love is the framework within which the requirement to practice justice is always to be located."[69]

Though at times it seems that goodness has been defeated in our world, the task and vocation of humanity is not to turn away from the world, but to continue to embody, to enact, to watch over and to cherish the holiness of life in all its truth and goodness and beauty. In a way that is reminiscent of Julian of Norwich's testimony that "all will be well", Erazim Kohák believes that what survives the inexorable forces of time and history, and death and suffering is the absolute value of the Good. "Though we seldom acknowledge it amid the shipwrecks of life," writes Kohák, "love and hope continue to survive by clinging to an extreme confidence: *it will be all right*, whatever comes, unwanted, unacceptable, unavoidable, it will be all right, in ways that we may not be able to imagine or pray for, it will somehow be all right. We could not go on living if we ceased to believe that."[70] The poet and the saint are the ones who bear witness to life's inherent goodness and holiness – even, and perhaps especially, in times of darkness and despair. Kohák writes:

> It is those humans who are willing to suffer and to die – needlessly, as time judges need – so that the goodness, the truth and the beauty of the eternal, would not perish but would rise to eternal validity. It is Václav Benda, recently released after surviving a four-year prison term because he refused to collaborate with the political police, saying simply, "There is this commandment, 'Thou shalt not bear false witness.'" It is all those who choose to live in truth, [including] the millions of nameless, unnoted others who have suffered and died – and often far less dramatically, who have *lived* – so that the good, the true, the beautiful will not dissipate unnoted into the cosmos. They are the salt of the earth…It is they who remind us of the full and specific sense of our humanity and our place in the cosmos, as the beings who,

living at the intersection of time and eternity, can bring the eternal into time – and raise time to eternity.[71]

One of the great tasks of a holy life is to bear witness to the *via superlativa* of God's overflowing love. God is not so much the "Wholly Other" that exists in some transcendent realm apart from our lives. Rather, transcendence is "excedence" or "surplus" or "more than" – there is always more that I can know, more that I can love, more that I can cherish. This desire does not so much emerge from a lack – a *via negativa* – but from a positive overflowing, a surplus, a *via superlativa*.[72]

However, this is something we have to learn. It is not immediately apparent that human beings are drawn by God toward goodness. It is a great learning and a great understanding to know that we live in God and God's love, and that God sustains us in this love because of his commitment to creation. To see the *goodness* in which we are created helps us to more "naturally" align ourselves with this goodness and this grace, so that we can, as Jean Vanier suggests, "*become* human".[73]

The Midrash takes up an image from the Song of Songs, calling God's "Law of Life" a "hedge of lilies" (Song 7:3). The boundaries of God's Law are not harsh or strict; rather they are as soft as lilies. The Law's ethical teachings are "a hedge of flowers bordering a garden path – cultivated for the beauty they impart to a way of life cherished for its lovely blossoms and sweet fruit".[74] The Torah is a law of life that is rich in the sweet fruits of kindness, love and mercy. "God's law *is* mercy," Abraham Heschel says, and "God's mercy *is* law."[75]

The experience of injustice is, among other things, the experience of a wound. It is an experience of alienation or disharmony, a rift or rupture of relationships – from God who creates and loves us, from our fellow human beings, from ourselves. "The afflicted are overwhelmed with evil and starving for good," writes Simone Weil.[76] Injustice severs the "vital law of life" that seeks the peace and wellbeing of all of creation.

Both the Jewish and Christian traditions are intimately aware of the world's brokenness. Both know of God's suffering in the passion of a suffering people – the "little ones" and the "forgotten ones" – the "orphans, widows and strangers" (Isa. 1:17). The Christian tradition knows of this brokenness in the *via dolorosa* or the "way of sorrows" – the *via crucis*. On the night before he delivered his inaugural lecture in Paris (March 1256), the young Aquinas prayed: "Save me, Lord; I am going down among the children of men where your truths are smashed to bits" ("Salva me, Domine, quoniam diminutae sunt veritates inter filios hominum").[77] Aquinas believed that all of creation is drawn and magnetised by God's creative goodness. Yet he also knew that the world is cracked and broken by sin. Our task is to restore the original goodness of God's creation, to mend what is broken and to heal what is damaged.

In the Jewish tradition, the Kabbalah suggests that each person has the inherent capacity to affect the life of God. Every proper word and deed releases divine energy, while every improper action serves to reinforce the disunity with divine life. Humanity's "fallenness" has caused an injury to God, and only shards of divine light remain in the world. Earthly deeds stimulate or arouse divine life in such a way as to cause energy from the upper world to descend to the lower world. Merciful love and good deeds are vehicles for "repairing" (*tikkun*) divine life and enabling divine abundance to flow back to the lower realm.[78]

The dividing line between good and evil runs through each of us. Jewish philosopher Emmanuel Levinas suggests that this fault line is as "old as the world". Perhaps this is what the Christian tradition means by "original sin". However, Levinas suggests that there is also an "original goodness" that is as old as the world. He refers to this goodness as "being for the other". Rather than seizing my rights and claiming my place under the sun, Levinas prefers to speak of my existence as indebted and responsible to the other. Existence *for itself* is not the ultimate meaning of life; rather, it is existence *for the other*.[79]

One of Levinas's most difficult thoughts is that being-for-the-other extends even to accepting responsibility for the sin and persecution in the world that I did not commit. Being-for-the-other cannot simply mean that we "love those who love us" (Matt. 5:46). Levinas probes more deeply and in his Talmudic commentary titled "As Old as the World" he asks us to consider the ways in which "I can be responsible for that which I did not do and take upon myself a distress which is not mine". Responsibility for the other extends even as far as bearing responsibility for the sins you did not commit. "For the other" becomes "for the fault of the other", taking on the sin of the other, "which wants absolutely and unto death to substitute itself for the other – for his sin and his distress" – as though it were my own. If we ask: is this love that gives itself, even in taking on the sin and fault of the other, "as old as the world"? – Levinas replies, "for the human world to be possible…at each moment there must be someone who can be responsible for the other."[80]

In the Christian tradition, the events of Good Friday represent this mystery of "expiation" or "substitution". Christ dies *pro nobis* – *for us* and for the sake of our salvation. "Ours were the sufferings he bore, ours the sorrows he carried" (Isa. 53:4). As Hans Urs von Balthasar notes, on Good Friday "there is in the suffering of the living Jesus the readiness to drink the 'chalice' of wrath, that is, to let the whole power of sin spend its fury on him: he takes on the blows and the hate contained in it…" And on Holy Saturday "there is the descent of the dead Jesus to hell, his solidarity in the period of nontime [sic] with those who have lost their way from God…He is dead together with them…He enters into solidarity with those damning themselves".[81] "Surrendering himself to death, letting himself be taken for a sinner, he was bearing the faults of many" (Isa. 53:12).

The mysticism of Christianity suggests that if we "live in

The Beatitude of Mercy: Love Watches over Justice

Christ", then we too must bear the sins of others, we too must suffer the effects of human hatred, we too must take sin into our flesh – renouncing violence, renouncing hatred, renouncing all the ways that humanity deals in death. When we love each other, we must necessarily suffer each other's fault and undergo each other's sin, in forgiveness and forbearance, upholding rather than condemning each other in our shared humanity.

Solidarity is perhaps the word that comes closest to mercy. The word "merciful" is derived from "suffering with" the fate of another's misery; from this *misericordia* is named, since the misery of the suffering person makes the merciful person's heart suffer, *miserum cor*.[82] Mercy means that I stand in solidarity with the one who suffers, that I stand in solidarity with God who loves, that I stand in solidarity with "sinners" who are, like myself, always dependent on a love that outstrips judgement and is even stronger than death. Aquinas writes:

> A person is said to be merciful [*misericors*] as being sorrowful at heart [*miserum cor*]; in other words, as being affected with sorrow at the misery of another as though it were his own. Hence it follows that he endeavors to dispel the misery of this other, as if it were his own; and this is the effect of mercy.[83]

Taking on the suffering and sorrow of another "as though it were my own" expresses the conviction that we are bound together as human beings – in our joys and our hopes, and also in our sin and our distress.[84] If you pierce any human heart, it will bleed, as did Christ's sacred heart. "For the other" is "for the joy of the other" and also "for the fault of the other". "For the other" descends all the way to hell and ascends all the way to heaven. St Bernard of Clairvaux writes:

> The merciful quickly grasp the truth in their neighbours when their heart goes out to them with a love that unites them so closely that they feel their neighbours' good and ill as if it were

their own. "They rejoice with those who rejoice and weep with those who weep" (Rom 12:15). Their hearts are made more clear-sighted by love. It is fellow sufferers that readily feel compassion for the sick and the hungry.[85]

Merciful deeds are works that God loves; they divinise those who practise them and form them into the likeness of divine goodness. Mercy is an act of healing and love. It is healing because it seeks to help those in its care realise that we need not be condemned to hatred – love is possible. We need not be condemned to cycles of violence – forgiveness is possible. We need not be condemned to conflict and division – understanding is possible.

"I have come for those who are sick," Jesus said (Matt. 9:12). I have come as one "who serves" (Luke 22:27). According to its Latin roots, to give service (*ministratio*) is the "application or ministration of remedies". Theology, in this sense, is a healing discipline, and not merely (or only) a critical one. It is creative and restorative. It moves within the realms of joyous, sorrowful and glorious mysteries, while all the time seeking the "ministratio" or healing of God's goodness and mercy.

Works of Mercy

We are increasingly aware today of the role that social sin and structural factors play in the suffering of society. A typical distinction is drawn between "acts of charity" and "acts of justice". According to this distinction, acts of justice are associated with public actions that work for systemic change within larger social systems (e.g. political and economic structures) in order to transform the root causes of injustice. Acts of charity are associated with the need for immediate attention and relief for those who suffer the effects of social injustice, providing direct services such as food, clothing, shelter and so on.

Rather than speak of acts of justice or acts of charity, an early Christian tradition draws a distinction between the "corporal works of mercy" and the "spiritual works of mercy".[86] The seven corporal works of mercy are based on the passage from Isaiah that speaks of "the fasting that pleases God" (Isa. 58:6–10) and Jesus' parable of the Last Judgement (Matt. 25:34–40). The corporal works of mercy are very similar to what we call "acts of charity" – to feed the hungry, to give drink to the thirsty, to clothe the naked, to shelter the homeless, to visit the sick, to visit those in prison, to bury the dead. The spiritual works of mercy are to admonish the sinner, to instruct the ignorant, to counsel the doubtful, to comfort the sorrowful, to bear wrongs patiently, to forgive all injuries, and to pray for the living and the dead.

The familiar criticism of charity and the works of mercy is that they may distract morally committed people from the task of working for justice in the world, such that charity and works of mercy seem to treat symptoms of injustice while overlooking systemic causes. As Daniel Bell notes, under the pressure of modernity, which tends to privatise and individualise such works, practices like feeding the hungry, sheltering the stranger, comforting the sorrowful and bearing wrongs patiently hardly appear to challenge larger social systems and are often critiqued for leaving unjust structures largely untouched and intact.[87] The sovereignty of the ideas of justice, freedom and equality are especially revered in our secular age. They often require an allegiance of our minds and hearts that mirrors the devotion we once offered to God. The social and civic-minded individual has become the new emblem of a just society, freed of prejudice, tolerant, liberal and the very guarantor of enlightened reason and the cause of justice in the world.[88] In this scenario, justice is too often lauded as a political and social virtue and charity is reduced to a private and personal virtue oriented to immediate needs. Yet it would be a false charity that refuses to become engaged in the needs of human communities and their social problems.

With a little renewed imagination, it is possible to see how communities that are engaged in works of mercy are challenging systemic issues. Indeed, where Christian communities are so engaged, they are clearly political and clearly confronting structural and systemic realities. They are challenging a society of competitiveness, covetousness and possession with acts of solidarity, communal care and sharing. They are challenging market-based economies with cooperative economies based on the "common wealth". They are challenging a narrow focus on economic capital with a renewed focus on "social capital" and networks of communally engaged people. Communal works of mercy take a variety of forms – from small and local initiatives through to humanitarian organisations – they act as salt or leaven in society (Matt. 5:13; 13:33).

Charity and works of mercy do not preclude but rather demand resistance to social sin – one of the works of mercy, for example, is "admonishing sinners". Such admonishment may take the form of underlining that there is a lack of mercy in every act of injustice. The unjust are always at the same time the merciless, for they fail to feel the bonds of divine compassion and human solidarity.

It may seem that acts of justice have an advantage over acts of mercy. After all, we can plan and organise for justice. We can organise a community into action; we can challenge unjust laws; we can enact new and improved laws; we can raise critical voices and revise policies and practices. Acts of mercy, however, are not so "plan-able". It is rarely within the purview of a society to organise or legislate for mercy. Mercy can never be a wholly structured or institutionalised event. Does this mean that works of mercy can only ever remain marginal and relatively ineffective within the structures of society? Mercy has long-suffered these taunts – that it is a "weak" and under-developed practice that has little effect on the powers-that-be. However, as Mary's *Magnificat* testifies, mercy outlives all the powers-that-be (Luke 1: 46-56). It may seem that mercy only ever appears as lowliness and weakness – "poor as I am, small as I am" – yet mercy is born of infinite patience and knows that, in the end, only love is the measure of all things (1 Cor. 13:13). Mercy is from "age to age" and reminds us that justice alone can never be the sole value and measure of all things. Perhaps it is a blessing in disguise that mercy isn't ultimately tied to or bound by our systems and structures. Mercy often operates aside from or along the edges of these structures with ever-watchful eyes, refusing to allow the rule of justice to rule over everything.

While mercy and forgiveness are not the normal currency of political discourse, there are, nevertheless, examples of social mercy or social healing. "Social inclusion" is perhaps one example of social mercy finding expression within the political fabric of society. Social inclusion is a national priority for the current Australian government, and has also featured in the United Kingdom and many European Union countries, though less so in the United States.[89] Social inclusion recognises that "not everyone begins at the same starting point and some people strike setbacks or crises during their lives".[90] It recognises that many people face formidable obstacles in life that are not of their own making. "They are caught in a spiral of disadvantage from which they find it difficult to break free, no matter how hard they struggle."[91] Sometimes whole neighbourhoods or communities face setbacks and disadvantages in disproportionate measures. Social inclusion is an effort to reach out to those on the margins of society, to offer assistance and support so that they may participate in society's wellbeing. Economic growth alone is not enough and increased bureaucracy is not the answer. By reaching out to these struggling members of our society, social inclusion is an example of social mercy that responds to the multiple and cumulative barriers that face so many who are deprived and disadvantaged in our communities.

Another well known example of social mercy and social healing is South Africa's post-Apartheid Truth and Reconciliation Commission. Though not perfect, it nevertheless demonstrates that a social context can be nurtured to advance a communal process that seeks a "healing of breaches, the restoration of broken relationships, a seeking to rehabilitate both the victim and the perpetrator".[92] This is an attempt to enact "spiritual work" at the level of social organisation – employing the symbols, language and politics of a society to create an alternative environment that allows for the possibility of social healing. "This is a moral universe," writes Archbishop Desmond Tutu, "which means that despite all the evidence that seems to be to the contrary, there is no way that evil and injustice and oppression can have the last word…this is what upheld the morale of our people, to know that in the end good will prevail."[93] When goodness and mercy are intimately linked with justice, then social restoration has a greater chance of taking effect in the world, such that the conditions for social healing are made possible – or at least, conceivable. This is itself a small miracle in a world that too often flounders in its ability to even consider the socially healing capacities of merciful justice.

Near the end of his autobiography, *Long Walk to Freedom*, Nelson Mandela writes of his own desire – born of many years of struggle and imprisonment – to heal the cycles of violence that can so readily entrap human beings, to seek the freedom of the oppressor and the oppressed:

> It was during those long and lonely years in prison that my hunger for the freedom of my own people became a hunger for the freedom of all people, white and black. I knew as well as I knew anything that the oppressor must be liberated just as surely as the oppressed. When I walked out of prison, that was my mission, to liberate the oppressed and the oppressor both. Some say that has now been achieved. But I know that that is not the case…We have not taken the final step on our journey, but the first step on a longer and even more difficult road…
>
> I have walked that long road to freedom. I have tried not to falter; I have made missteps along the way. But I have discovered the secret that after climbing a great hill, one only finds that there are many more hills to climb. I have taken a moment here to rest, to steal a view of the glorious vista that surrounds me, to look back on the distance I have come. But I can only rest for a moment, for with freedom come responsibilities, and I dare not linger, for my long walk has not yet ended. [94]

In another time and another place, St Therese of Lisieux, affectionately known as "the little flower", wrote in her own diary that while justice ties us to the realms of the earth, mercy ascends all the way to the realms of heaven. "On all sides," she says, "God's merciful love is misunderstood and rejected." She counters the spectre of divine justice to the sphere of love's influence: "if your justice feels inclined to discharge itself, which, after all, *extends only over the earth*, how much more, then, does your merciful love yearn to inflame souls, because your mercy, after all, *ascends all the way to heaven*."[95]

Social Mercy and the "Little Act of Goodness"

"Politics left to itself," writes Emmanuel Levinas, "bears a tyranny within itself; it deforms the I and the other who have given rise to it, for it judges them according to universal rules, and thus *in absentia*."[96] The workings and determinations of justice are often conducted in the great halls of the law, in the manner of a "politics left to itself" and its own devices, as though politics had no other concern than its own concern, whereas all the time it should be concerned with the wellbeing of the *polis* and the common good. And all too often, rules and legislation and judgements are made in the absence of the one who stands outside – "in absentia" – as though the law didn't really care about those left standing outside its gates, whereas all the time it is meant to be concerned for the welfare of all, even and especially for the least of all.

Left to itself, the wheels of politics and the laws of justice can turn with unrelenting power – "oh, the violence of administration!" Levinas cries.[97] The processes and systems of management and regulation are everywhere in our lives. Knowingly or unknowingly, we are entangled in procedures of power, policy and paperwork. Hannah Arendt calls it our "infinitely complex red-tape existence".[98] In 2009 alone, more than 50,000 pages of new laws and regulations were enacted in Australia, such that we may well wonder what it means to say that we live in a free society.[99]

"Every attempt to organize humanity fails," writes Levinas.[100] Many a system has been tried, and many a system has failed. Even the much lauded system of "democracy" has not yet achieved what it seeks, as Martin Luther King's "I Have A Dream" speech at Washington D.C. powerfully attests.[101] "Is there a need to stress the possible ambiguity of every social ideology?" asks Pope Paul VI. He continues:

> Sometimes it leads political or social activity to be simply the application of an abstract, purely theoretical idea. There is also the danger of giving adherence to an ideology…to take refuge in it as a final and sufficient

> explanation of everything, and thus to build a new idol, accepting, at times without being aware of doing so, its totalitarian and coercive character. And people imagine they find in it a justification for their activity, even violent activity, and an adequate response to a desire to serve. The desire remains but it allows itself to be consumed by an ideology which, even if it suggests certain paths to man's liberation, ends up by making him a slave.[102]

Paul VI worries that "politics left to itself" holds the inherent danger, even under the banner of a desire to serve, of turning the law and politics into an idol. Even democracy can be turned into an idol as, for example, the way it is currently invoked by those who seek a justification for the "war on terror". Violence can spread even in the name of democracy and freedom, especially if these are taken as "a final and sufficient explanation of everything". Paul VI offers the following caution: "Politics are a demanding manner – but not the only one – of living the Christian commitment of service to others…The domain of politics is wide and comprehensive, but it is not exclusive. An attitude of encroachment which would tend to set up politics as an absolute value would bring serious danger."[103]

This is a concern that Levinas also shares, for he has personally witnessed and suffered the dangers of social and political systems that can all too easily assume the tyranny of coercive and totalitarian practices. Collective structures always harbour a tendency to forget or exclude or oppress the very relation that "gives rise" to political activity, namely, the "I and the other" of human fraternity and ethical responsibility. Levinas's insistence on the face-to-face relation is not an apolitical stance; rather, it is the very prompting of a transformed conception of politics and society, one that keeps before us the fundamental responsibility of the ethical relation, the face of the human other that is irreducible to any form of totalising politics.[104]

On its own, politics "deforms the I and the other". In other words, the ethical relation must continually inspire the social and political order. Paul VI writes:

> Human rights are still too often disregarded, if not scoffed at, or else they

receive only formal recognition. In many cases legislation does not keep up with real situations. Legislation is necessary, but it is not sufficient for setting up true relationships of justice and equality…If beyond legal rules, there is no deeper feeling of respect for and service to others, then even equality before the law can serve as an alibi for flagrant discrimination, continued exploitation, and actual contempt.[105]

One of the cardinal points of Catholic social teaching is that the human person "is the foundation, cause, and end of all social institutions".[106] While we must necessarily attend to the social fabric of our institutional structures, political administrations and judicial systems, we must recognise that all these social institutions are not so much the *foundation* or basis of ethical relations, but the *consequences* or "guardianships" of the more primary ethical relation that comes to us, not from our well constructed social theories or ethical codes, but from the fundamental relationship of the "I and the other". If our social and political frameworks are not directed toward or inspired by this fundamental ethical relation, then our "collective measures lose their human meaning because they have forgotten or masked real faces and real speech. This forgetfulness is the beginning of tyranny".[107]

The true aim of all social and political activity "should be to help individual members of the social body, but never to destroy or absorb them".[108] Levinas notes, however, that there is a "ceaseless deep remorse of justice",[109] for while the dignity of each and every person is *unique* and *incomparable*, there are nevertheless times when it is necessary for the law to calculate and make comparisons, to weigh and to measure. Justice that seeks to be true and good is always saddened by its inability to be truly just for each and every person who comes before the law, because it knows that it must necessarily weigh individual cases according to universal principles, and yet it also knows that no universal principle is ever adequate to deal with each and every human particularity that comes before it in all its special instance and circumstance. "Legislation is always unfinished, always resumed," Levinas says. While the law aims to approximate the justice due to every person, it is nevertheless "distanced by the necessary calculations imposed by a multiple sociality, calculations constantly starting over again".[110] In other words, the law – when it is functioning well or as best it can – is nevertheless painfully and "remorsefully" aware of its own pitfalls and shortcomings.

"Justice is necessary," Levinas says, "that is, comparison, coexistence, assembling, order, thematization…the intelligibility of a system, and thence also a copresence on an equal footing as before a court of justice."[111] However, this "reasonable justice" that is based on fairness and equality and universal principles, is nevertheless "bound by legal strictures and cannot equal the goodness that solicits and inspires it".[112] Underlying all quests for justice stands "the whole gravity of love" – a love that does not measure or boast; rather, a love that "bears all things" (1 Cor. 13:7). In the name of this love, Levinas prefers to "reserve another word: *miséricorde*, mercy, when one assumes responsibility for the suffering of another".[113] He even goes so far as to suggest that

> the little act of goodness *(la petite bonté)* from one person to their neighbour is lost and deformed as soon as it seeks organization and universality and system, as soon as it opts for doctrine, a treatise of politics, a party, a state, and even a church. Yet it remains the sole refuge of the good in being. Unbeaten, it undergoes violence and evil, which, as little goodness, it can neither vanquish nor drive out.[114]

"Justice itself is born of charity."[115] If it is inspired by goodness, if it is founded on charity, if it is chastened and softened by mercy, then it may be possible for justice to best approximate what it seeks. Otherwise, it will always be deformed and wounded, unable to hear the appeal of mercy that always wells up from the concern of one for another. "God is the God of justice, but his principle attribute is mercy."[116] Love disarms justice. Love unsettles justice. Love watches over justice.

According to Martha Nussbaum, a politics "inclined to mercy" recognises "how pervasive the obstacles to goodness are, how deeply rooted, how much a part of oneself as well as others". A politics of mercy diverges from strictness toward forbearance, from cruelty toward "a slow gentle fostering of what good there may be". A politics of mercy recognises that "the human world is held together by pity and fellow-feeling".[117]

Acts of charity and mercy may seem small and insignificant in the face of the huge demands of social justice and the necessary concerns of politics in the world. However, it is often these small and fragile acts of love that ultimately watch over justice. Just as the parent watches over their child who is sick, or the lover watches for their beloved, sitting up through the night – "faint with love" (Song 5:8) – unable to sleep but rather full of concern and solicitude, so too "love must watch over justice".[118] As Chappell suggests, "mercy not only crowns or seasons justice, but ultimately even supplants it".[119] The seemingly fragile acts of tenderness and love – acts of social mercy – should not be considered as mere "band-aids". Rather, they are the very sign of God's goodness in the world. A rabbinic parable speaks of the Messiah who is found at the city gates, attending to the afflicted and the suffering, "binding up their wounds", and says that while "others bind an *entire* area covering *several* wounds with one bandage, the Messiah dresses *each wound separately*".[120] Acts of mercy and charity may often appear as mere supplements to the grander works of justice; they may even appear as "foolish" in the eyes of the world, and yet St Paul says:

> God chose what is foolish in the world to shame the wise; God chose what is weak in the world to shame the strong; God chose what is low and despised in the world, things that are not, to reduce to nothing things that are…None of the rulers of this age have understood this. (1 Cor 1:27–18; 2:8).

"Various models have been tried," Paul VI says, "but none of them gives complete satisfaction." Nevertheless, "the Christian has the duty to take part in this search and in the organization and life of political society".[121] This leads me to wonder: must the practical and ethical sphere of society always operate under the auspices of justice? Or, as Paul Ricoeur suggests, along with the demands of justice, do we not also need a "poetics of love"?[122] Could it be that an "excess of justice" – lacking in love or mercy

– is dangerously close to becoming an injustice? On the other hand, is it possible that an "excess of love" could ever jeopardise or fail the requirements of justice? Isn't it rather, that the practices of love and mercy keep justice from becoming unjust, such that the conditions of justice are always tested against the superabundance of merciful and unconditional love? "Love – *caritas* – will always prove necessary," writes Pope Benedict XVI, "even in the most just society. There is no ordering of the State so just that it can eliminate the need for a service of love. Whoever wants to eliminate love is eliminating…the very thing that the suffering person – every person – needs: namely, loving personal concern."[123]

If we could be more aware of the need for social mercy, if we could speak more readily of social mercy, if we could let the language and the sentiments of social mercy hold greater sway in our society and our institutions and our social structures, we would in no way jeopardise our quest for social justice. Rather, we would enhance this quest. Mercy is the very foundation of justice, such that without social mercy, our quest for social justice will always be misguided and thwarted.

Mercy is "the sole refuge of the good in being". While justice is imperative – a debt, a mutual indebtedness – mercy remains as the sole refuge in life, the sole refuge in our relationships and our society. Mercy is a refuge for the immigrant, relief for the over-burdened and a rescue for the afflicted. Social mercy is crucial to our society; without it we could not even claim *to be* a society – a society, that is, of any human or humane proportion, where our bonds are always ones of friendship and fraternity, forgiveness and forbearance – knowing that we are all in this boat together, and only mercy can sustain us.

ENDNOTES

[1] St. Augustine, *Exposition on the Book of Psalms*, Ps. XXXIII, 10, on v.5.

[2] Martha C. Nussbaum, *Love's Knowledge: Essays on Philosophy and Literature* (New York: Oxford University Press, 1990).

[3] An earlier version of this essay appeared in my book, *Practical Theology: On Earth as It Is in Heaven* (Maryknoll, NY: Orbis Books, 2005), Chapter 10.

[4] Pope Paul VI, *Octogesima Adveniens: A Call to Action on the Eightieth Anniversary of Rerum Novarum* (Vatican City, 1971), no. 12. Retrieved from the Vatican Web site: www.vatican.va. Throughout this essay I have not adapted quotations for inclusive language but have left them in their original wording.

[5] Michael A. Cowan and Bernard J. Lee, *Conversation, Risk & Conversion: The Inner and Public Lives of Small Christian Communities* (Maryknoll, NY: Orbis Books, 1997), 117.

[6] Ibid., 120.

[7] Pope John XXIII, *Pacem in Terris: Peace on Earth* (Vatican City, 1963). Retrieved from the Vatican Web site: www.vatican.va.

[8] Franz Kafka, *Franz Kafka: The Complete Stories*, ed. Nahum N. Glatzer (New York: Schocken Books, 1971), 3-4.

[9] United States Conference of Catholic Bishops, *Economic Justice for All* (U.S. Catholic Bishops, 1986), no. 87. Retrieved from the United States Conference of Catholic Bishops Web site: www.usccb.org.

[10] Ibid., no. 88.

[11] Gustavo Gutiérrez, *Essential Writings*, ed. James B. Nickoloff (Minneapolis: Fortress Press, 1996), 144-145.

[12] Ibid.,128.

[13] Paul Ricoeur, *Oneself as Another*, trans. Kathleen Blamey (Chicago: The University of Chicago Press, 1992), 354.

[14] *Catechism of the Catholic Church*, no. 2446. Retrieved from the Vatican Web site: www.vatican.va

[15] Ibid.

[16] Pope John Paul II, *Sollicitudo Rei Socialis: On Social Concern* (Vatican City, 1987), no. 47. Retrieved from the Vatican Web site: www.vatican.va

[17] Ibid., 323 (Italics mine).

[18] Pope John Paul II, *Dives In Misericordia: Rich in Mercy* (Sydney: St Pauls Publications, 1980), 64.

[19] Ibid., 65.

[20] Ibid.

[21] Ibid., 77-78.

[22] Simone Weil, "Human Personality" in *Simone Weil: An Anthology*, ed. Sian Miles (London: Penguin Books, 2005), 93.

[23] Ibid., 81.

[24] Simone Weil, *Waiting on God: Letters and Essays*, trans. Emma Crauford (London: Fount/HarperCollins, 1977), 141.

[25] Simone Weil, "Human Personality", 72.

[26] Jacques Derrida, "Force of the Law: The 'Mystical Foundation of Authority'" in Drucilla Cornell, Michel Rosenfeld, David Gray Carlson, eds, *Deconstruction and the Possibility of Justice* (New York: Routledge, 1992), 14.

[27] Jacques Derrida and John Caputo, *Deconstruction in a Nutshell: A Conversation with Jacques Derrida* (New York: Fordham University Press, 1997), 16-17.

[28] This is a familiar strategy in Derrida's work. He takes sizeable words such as "justice," "gift," "hospitality" and "forgiveness" and tries to show that these are inherently unrealisable and impossible, yet this impossibility keeps us alert to false "fulfilments" and prompts us to continually seek their expression.

[29] Leonard Cohen, "That Don't Make It Junk," from the CD *Ten New Songs* (Sony Music, 2001).

[30] See Søren Kierkegaard's reflection, "Mercifulness, a Work of Love, Even if It Can Give Nothing and is Capable of Doing Nothing", Chapter VII in *Works of Love* (New York: Harper & Row, 1962).

[31] K.E. Løgstrup, *Beyond the Ethical Demand* (Notre Dame, IN: University of Notre Dame Press, 2007), 79.

[32] Jon Sobrino, *The Principle of Mercy: Taking the Crucified People from the Cross* (Maryknoll, NY: Orbis Books, 1994), 18.

[33] Ibid.

[34] Pope John Paul II, *Dives In Misericordia: Rich in Mercy*, 68.

[35] Jon Sobrino, *The Principle of Mercy*, 15-16.

[36] Ibid., 17-19 (commenting on the Parable of the Good Samaritan).

[37] K.E. Løgstrup, *Beyond the Ethical Demand*, 77.

[38] Heather Chappell, "*Conversion By Mercy* and *For A Praxis of Mercy*", paper presented at the 2001 convention of the Catholic Theological Society of America, 5.

[39] Pope John Paul II, *Dives In Misericordia: Rich in Mercy*, 39.

[40] Ibid., 73-74.

[41] Heather Chappell, "*Conversion By Mercy*", 6.

[42] Edward Schillebeeckx, *Jesus: An Experiment in Christology* (New York: Crossroad, 1991), 165-166.

[43] Heather Chappell, "*Conversion By Mercy*", 6.

[44] *Pesachim* 54a. My thanks to Rabbi Barry Leff for this reference.

[45] Adin Steinsaltz, *The Thirteen Petalled Rose*, trans. Yehuda Hanegbi (Lanham, Maryland: A Jason Aronson Book, Rowman & Littlefield Publishers, 1992), 125.

[46] Hannah Arendt, "Labor, Work, Action" in *The Portable Hannah Arendt*, ed. Peter Baehr (New York: Penguin Books, 2000), 181.

[47] Ibid.

[48] Ibid.

[49] John Caputo, *Against Ethics: Contributions to a Poetics of Obligation with Constant Reference to Deconstruction* (Bloomington: Indiana University Press, 1993), 111-112.

[50] *Brachot* 7a. My thanks to Rabbi Barry Leff for providing this text.

[51] At its root, *rahamim* denotes the love of a mother (*rehem*, "mother's womb"). Jesus is referred to as "the fruit of the womb" (Luke 1:42). See J. Sheila Galligan, "Mercy's Mystery: Womb-like Love", *Spiritual Life* (Spring 2010), 49-55.

[52] Henryk Mikolaj Górecki, "Miserere: Opus 44", from the CD *Miserere*

(Elektra Entertainment, 1994).

53 Edward Schillebeeckx, *Church: The Human Story of God* (New York: Crossroad, 1990), 6.

54 Walter Benjamin, "Modernism," in *Poetry in Theory*, edited by Jon Cook (Oxford: Blackwell Publishing, 2004), citing Péguy, 230.

55 Pope John Paul II, *Dives In Misericordia: Rich in Mercy*, 49.

56 Ibid., 74.

57 Ibid., 28.

58 Ibid., 50, 75.

59 Ibid., 76.

60 Lawrence Fine, "Kabbalistic Texts", in Barry W. Holtz, ed. *Back to the Sources: Reading the Classic Jewish Texts* (New York: Simon and Schuster, 1984), 322. Hesed – "lovingkindness" – occurs 245 times in the Hebrew Bible, 26 times in Psalm 136 alone.

61 Fine, "Kabbalistic Texts", 323.

62 Miroslav Volf, *Exclusion and Embrace: A Theological Exploration of Identity, Otherness and Reconciliation* (Nashville: Abingdon Press, 1996), 217.

63 Fine, "Kabbalistic Texts", 323.

64 Simone Weil, "Human Personality", 93.

65 Daniel M. Bell, Jr., "Sacrifice and Suffering: Beyond Justice, Human Rights, and Capitalism" in *Modern Theology* 18:3 (July 2002), 334, 350.

66 On the relationship between love and justice in the works of Aquinas (and Julian of Norwich), see Ellen Charry, *By the Renewing of Your Minds: The Pastoral Function of Christian Doctrine* (New York: Oxford University Press, 1997), Chapter 8. On the themes of love, justice and friendship in Thomas Aquinas, see Thomas L. Schubeck, *Love That Does Justice* (Maryknoll, NY: Orbis Books, 2007), Ch. 5.

67 Daniel M. Bell, Jr., "Sacrifice and Suffering", 336.

68 Thomas Aquinas, *Summa Theologica* 1, question 21, articles 3-4.

69 Gustavo Gutiérrez, *On Job: God-Talk and the Suffering of the Innocent* (Maryknoll: Orbis Books, 1987), 89.

70 Erazim Kohák, *The Embers and the Stars: A Philosophical Inquiry into the Moral Sense of Nature* (Chicago: University of Chicago Press, 1984), 162.

[71] Ibid., 102.

[72] Susan A. Handelman, *Fragments of Redemption: Jewish Thought and Literary Theory in Benjamin, Schoelm, and Levinas* (Bloomington: Indiana University Press, 1991), 197.

[73] Jean Vanier, *Becoming Human* (New York: Paulist Press, 1998).

[74] See *Song of Songs Rabbah* 7:3.2. The reference is cited in Lenn E. Goodman, *Love Thy Neighbor As Thyself* (Oxford: Oxford University Press, 2008), 65-66.

[75] Abraham Heschel, *Man is Not Alone: A Philosophy of Religion* (New York: Farrar, Straus & Giroux, 1976), 118.

[76] Simone Weil, "Human Personality", 86.

[77] Marie-Dominique Chenu, *Aquinas and His Role in Theology* (Collegeville: Liturgical Press, 2002), 45.

[78] Fine, "Kabbalistic Texts", 327-329; Daniel Matt, *The Essential Kabbalah* (San Francisco: HarperSanFrancisco, 1996), 15.

[79] Richard A. Coehen, ed., *Face to Face with Emmanuel Levinas* (Albany: State University of New York Press, 1986), 24.

[80] Emmanuel Levinas, *Nine Talmudic Readings*, trans. Annette Aronowicz (Bloomington: Indiana University Press, 1990). The references in this paragraph are from pp. 85-86.

[81] Hans Urs von Balthasar, *The Von Balthasar Reader*, eds Medard Kehl and Werner Loser, trans. Robert Daly and Fred Lawrence (New York: Crossroad Publishing Company), 153.

[82] My thanks to Dr Bronwen Neil from the Centre for Early Christian Studies, Australian Catholic University, for her assistance with this Latin translation.

[83] Aquinas, *Summa Theologica* 1, question 21, article 3.

[84] *Gaudium et Spes: Pastoral Constitution on the Church in the Modern World* (Second Vatican Council, 1965), no. 1. Retrieved from the Vatican Web site: www.vatican.va.

[85] St. Bernard of Clairvaux, *The Steps of Humility and Pride*, trans. M. Ambrose Conway (Kalamazoo: Cistercian Publications, 1989), 34.

[86] *Catechism of the Catholic Church*, no. 2447.

[87] Daniel M. Bell, Jr, "Forgiveness and the End of Economy" in *Studies in*

Christian Ethics 20:3 (2007), 341-43.

[88] Wayne Cristaudo, "Love and the Limits of Justice" in *Power, Love and Evil: Contribution to a Philosophy of the Damaged* (Amsterdam: Rodopi, 2008), 116.

[89] Alan Hayes, Matthew Gray and Ben Edwards, *Social Inclusion: Origins, Concepts and Key Themes* (Social Inclusion Unit, Department of the Prime Minister and Cabinet, Commonwealth of Australia, October 2008), 4-6, 9-12. Further resources are available at www.socialinclusion.gov.au.

[90] *A Stronger, Fairer Australia: A New Social Inclusion Strategy* (Social Inclusion Unit, Department of the Prime Minister and Cabinet, Commonwealth of Australia, 2009), 1.

[91] Ibid., 8.

[92] Desmond Tutu, *No Future Without Forgiveness* (New York: Doubleday, 1999), 55. Other examples can be found in Priscilla Hayner, *Unspeakable Truths: Facing the Challenge of Truth Commissions* (New York: Routledge, 2002). See also the reflections offered in Robert Schreiter, *The Ministry of Reconciliation: Spirituality and Strategies* (Maryknoll: Orbis Books, 1998). Kaye Reid also makes creative connections between South Africa's Commission and the Christian theology of *kenosis* in her MA Thesis, "Kenosis as a gift to humanity of God's grace to be lived relationally" (Melbourne College of Divinity, December, 2009).

[93] Desmond Tutu, *Believe* (Sydney: Hachette Australia, 2007), 26.

[94] Nelson Mandela, *Long Walk To Freedom* (London: Abacus, 1994), 751.

[95] Therese of Lisieux, *Autobiography of a Saint*, Book 1, Chapter XXIX.

[96] Emmanuel Levinas, *Totality and Infinity: An Essay in Exteriority*, trans. Alphonso Lingis (Pittsburgh: Duquesne University Press, 1969), 300.

[97] Emmanuel Levinas, *Is It Righteous To Be? Interviews with Emmanuel Levinas*, ed. Jill Robbins (Stanford: Stanford University Press, 2001), 51.

[98] Hannah Arendt, *The Portable Hannah Arendt*, 25.

[99] Robin Speed, "The Rise and Rise of the Regulators" *The Australian Newspaper* (Friday, January 15, 2009).

[100] Emmanuel Levinas, *Is It Righteous To Be?*, 217.

[101] Martin Luther King, *A Testament of Hope: The Essential Writings and Speeches of Martin Luther King* (New York: HarperSanFrancisco, 1986), 217-220.

[102] Pope Paul VI, *Octogesima Adveniens: A Call to Action*, nos. 27-28.

[103] Ibid., no. 46.

[104] Emmanuel Levinas, "Peace and Proximity" in *Basic Philosophical Writings*, eds. Adriaan T. Peperzak, Simon Critchley and Robert Bernasconi (Bloomington: Indiana University Press, 1996), 161-69.

[105] Pope Paul VI, *Octogesima Adveniens: A Call to Action*, no. 23.

[106] Pope John XXIII, *Mater et Magistra: Christianity and Social Progress* (Vatican City, 1961), no. 219. Retrieved from the Vatican Web site: www.vatican.va

[107] Adriaan Peperzak, *To The Other: An Introduction to the Philosophy of Emmanuel Levinas* (West Lafayette: Purdue University Press, 1993), 31.

[108] Pope Paul VI, *Octogesima Adveniens: A Call to Action*, no. 46.

[109] Emmanuel Levinas, *Is It Righteous to Be?*, 206.

[110] Ibid.

[111] Emmanuel Levinas, *Otherwise Than Being or Beyond Essence*, trans. Alphonso Lingis (Dordrecht: Kluwer Academic Publishers, 1991), 157.

[112] Emmanuel Levinas, *Is It Righteous To Be?*, 207.

[113] Ibid., 146.

[114] Ibid., 206-07.

[115] Ibid., 168.

[116] Ibid., 169.

[117] Martha C. Nussbaum, *Love's Knowledge*, 213, 375.

[118] Emmanuel Levinas, *Is It Righteous To Be?*, 169.

[119] Heather Chappell, "Conversion By Mercy", 14.

[120] Chaim Pearl, *Theology in Rabbinic Stories* (Peabody, Mass: Hendrickson Publishers, 1997), 145 (citing *Sanhedrin* 98a). Italics mine.

[121] Pope Paul IV, *Octogesima Adveniens: A Call to Action*, no. 24.

[122] Paul Ricoeur, "Love and Justice" in *Figuring the Sacred: Religion, Narrative, and Imagination* (Minneapolis: Fortress Press, 1995), 315-29.

[123] Pope Benedict XVI, *Deus Caritas Est: God is Love* (Sydney: St. Pauls Publications, 2006), 45-46.

The Beatitude of Mercy: Love Watches over Justice

www.ingramcontent.com/pod-product-compliance
Lightning Source LLC
LaVergne TN
LVHW081355060426
835510LV00013B/1838